AN ADDISONIAN PRESS BOOK

Fishes Dangerous to Man

ALAN MARK FLETCHER
ILLUSTRATED BY
JANE TEIKO OKA
AND WILLI BAUM

ADDISON-WESLEY

Addisonian Press Books by Alan Mark Fletcher
FISHES DANGEROUS TO MAN
FISHES THAT HIDE
FISHES THAT TRAVEL
FISHES AND THEIR YOUNG

J
597.06
FLE

Text Copyright © 1969 by Alan Mark Fletcher
Text Philippines Copyright © 1969 by Alan Mark Fletcher
Illustrations Copyright © 1969 by Jane Teiko Oka and Willi Baum
Illustrations Philippines Copyright © 1969 by Jane Teiko Oka and Willi Baum
All Rights Reserved.
Addison-Wesley Publishing Company, Inc.
Reading, Massachusetts 01867
Library of Congress Catalog Card No. 71-80502
ISBN: 0-201-02056-4
Printed in the United States of America

ABCDEFGHIJK-WZ-79876

CONTENTS

4

To Ruth and Paul

Most fishes are harmless to man. Many kinds are useful to humans in different ways. However, a few kinds are dangerous to man in one way or another. These are the ones we will talk about in this book.

CHAPTER ONE

Electric Eel

Maria is an Indian girl who lives with her family along a small river in a very wild part of South America. Like all Indian children, Maria has chores to do every day. One of Maria's chores is to keep the water bucket full. Two or three times each day she carries the bucket down to the river, walks out to the deep part where the water is cleaner, and fills the bucket. Then she places the bucket on her head, walks up to the hut, climbs the stairs, and puts the heavy bucket on the shelf in the kitchen—all without spilling a drop.

One day Maria filled the bucket in the river as she had done hundreds of times before, but as she began to walk out, she screamed and dropped the bucket. Then she fell unconscious in the water.

When her father heard the scream, he ran out to Maria. He dragged her in to shore, and for a few moments he was terribly frightened. Maria was not breathing. Finally she began to breathe again, very slowly. In a few minutes she opened her eyes weakly. Maria was sick for several days, but she did get well.

What had happened was no mystery to Maria's father. He knew at once that Maria had brushed against a large electric eel, one of the most fearsome fishes in the world.

Surely the electric eel of South America is one of the most ugly of fishes. It looks like a dark brown snake, with one continuous fin running along most of its under side. Two small, beady eyes look out from a rounded head.

Electric eels have special organs which can produce powerful electrical shocks. A six-foot eel, for example, can produce about 500 volts of electricity. That voltage is almost five times as powerful as the electricity that flows through the wires in your home.

No wonder Maria was knocked unconscious! She was lucky to be alive.

It is only by accident that people get shocked by electric eels. The eel's electricity is used in getting food, and people are not on the menu. The electric eel feeds on other water animals, mostly fishes. When hungry it brushes up against another fish, giving it a powerful shock. While the fish is still unconscious the electric eel quickly eats it.

Several other fishes are known to produce electricity. The electric catfish of Africa and different kinds of electric rays, especially the kind found off the coast of Florida, can cause a painful shock. However, the electric eel is by far the most powerful shocking animal in the world.

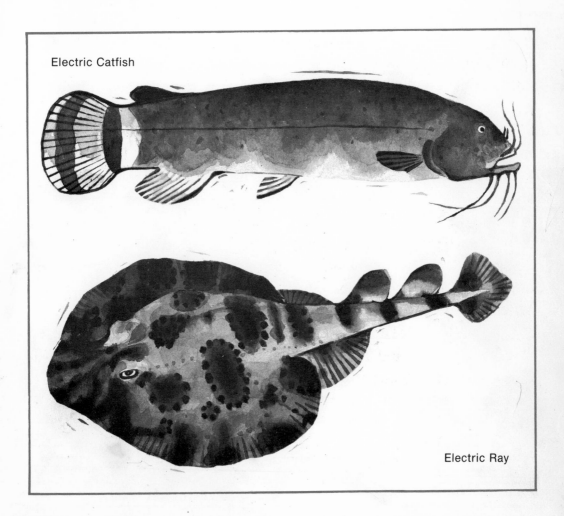

Electric Catfish

Electric Ray

CHAPTER TWO

Great White Shark

Have you ever been swimming at the seashore when someone cried, "Shark, shark!"? Few animals strike so much fear in the hearts of people as do sharks. The cry "Shark, Shark!" sends bathers scurrying out of the water as fast as their legs can carry them.

Of the 250 or so kinds of sharks, only a few are dangerous to man, although many kinds have sharp, ugly teeth. In parts of the world that have cold winters, sharks usually become a problem only when the water grows warm in the summer. Then sharks often move from their tropical homes to temperate regions. This is also the time when people like to swim. Shark attacks on people are rare, but every summer a few cases are reported in the newspapers.

Probably the best known and most widely feared is the great white shark. It is often called "the man-eater." Great white sharks grow to a length of thirty feet. They are very heavy fish, too. A 15-footer will weigh about 2,500 pounds.

Great white sharks are found in tropical waters throughout the world. During the summer months they often move into the temperate regions. Fortunately for bathers, great white sharks do not often come into shallow water. However, attacks on people have occurred as far north in the Atlantic Ocean as Buzzard's Bay, Massachusetts, and in the Pacific Ocean along the California coast.

The mako shark is a much smaller fish, growing to 15 feet. It, too, is considered to be very dangerous. It is found in warm waters all over the world, including the coasts of the United States during the summer. The mako is a very fast swimmer.

Tiger sharks are widely feared as man-eaters. In fact, they will eat almost anything. Fishes, crabs, birds, garbage, tin cans, and parts of people have been found in tiger shark stomachs. Tiger sharks grow to about 20 feet and can weigh nearly 2,000 pounds. They are found mostly in the tropics, but in the summertime they have been caught as far north in the Atlantic as Long Island.

One of the strangest-looking fishes in the world is the hammerhead shark, which grows to a length of about 12 feet. The sides of the head of a large hammerhead may stick out as far as 36 inches. An eye and a nostril are on each end of the sides that stick out. The hammerhead is another tropical shark that often moves into temperate regions when the weather becomes warm in the summer. All doubt

Hammerhead Shark

Tiger Shark

about the hammerhead being dangerous to man was removed a long time ago when parts of a human body were removed from the stomach of a large one caught off Long Island.

All sharks, except one kind, live in the oceans. The one kind of fresh-water shark lives in Lake Nicaragua, Central America. Scientists believe that many ages ago some sharks swam from the ocean up the San Carlos River into Lake Nicaragua. Then the course of the river changed so that the sharks could not return to the ocean. They survived in the lake, and now many of their descendants live there.

Lake Nicaragua sharks grow to about eight feet. Although small for sharks, they are still dangerous. Bathers in Lake Nicaragua have been bitten by them. Some people have even been killed.

Lake Nicaragua Fresh-water Shark

Piranhas

Piranha   Exposed Skeleton of Piranha

In the dark waters of South America's jungles there is another kind of biting fish. It is small, but it is much more dangerous to man than sharks are. With its razor-sharp teeth and very strong jaws, the piranha has bitten pieces from untold numbers of Indians.

Since the piranha seldom grows to be more than a foot long, people have wondered how it can be really dangerous to man and other large creatures. A piranha is able to take a nasty bite, but one bite is not likely to cause death. The real danger of piranhas is that where they are found there usually are hundreds of them. If an animal or a man

wanders into the water, one piranha takes a bite. The bleeding caused by the first bite excites the other piranhas. Soon all other piranhas for some distance around are thrashing about madly. If the victim is not able to get out of the water quickly, in a few minutes there is nothing left but a skeleton.

Piranhas are found throughout most of the northern half of South America. They are fresh-water fishes. While there are several different kinds, they all look very much alike, and they all have those fearsome, sharp teeth.

Perhaps the strangest thing about piranhas is that they are not always dangerous. In one river children may swim without ever being bitten while hundreds of piranhas are also swimming nearby.

In another river, only a few miles away, the same kind of piranhas may be so dangerous that a person in a canoe may lose a finger if he forgets and lets his hand trail in the water. Scientists who study piranhas have not been able to learn why piranhas are dangerous in one place and not in another.

Of course, piranhas do not depend on people as food. If they did, there would not be enough "human" food to feed the thousands of piranhas that are found in some rivers. The regular food of piranhas is other fishes. Sometimes piranhas even eat each other. Once in a while some wild animal, and more rarely a person, wanders into the water. Then the piranhas have a "tasty" change from their usual fish diet.

Until a few years ago, live piranhas were often brought back from South America for sale in tropical fish stores. Many aquarists had piranhas for pets in home aquariums. There was a grim pleasure in saying to friends, "See those fish in the aquarium? They are man-eating fish from the Amazon!" Then some people became afraid that piranhas might get loose in lakes and streams in the United States. So a law was passed forbidding collectors to bring them into the country for general sale. If you wish to see the little man-eaters today, you probably will have to look at them in a public aquarium, even though a few piranhas are sometimes shipped to pet stores by mistake.

Moray Eels

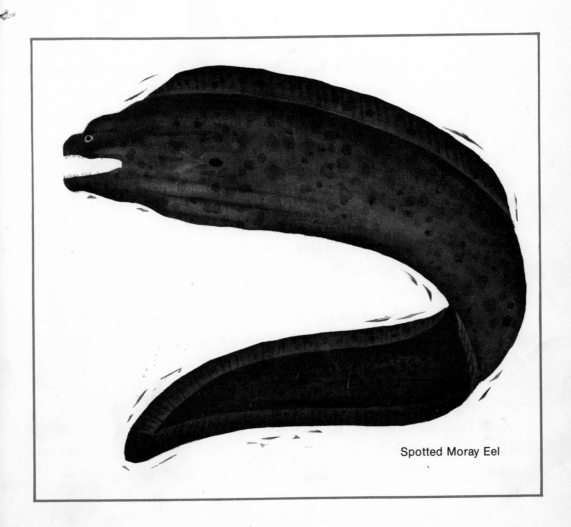

Spotted Moray Eel

24

Bill Hernandez is an expert skin diver. He is also an aquarist who enjoys collecting unusual fishes for his aquarium. He often combines the two hobbies by searching for fishes while he skin dives. One day he was swimming among coral growths, looking for small coral reef fishes. Bill spotted a deep, dark hole in the coral. "There might be some nice little fishes in there!" he said to himself. Holding his net near the hole with his left hand, he put his right hand into the hole to scare the fishes out. At once Bill's hand was grabbed by something in the dark hole. When he attempted to pull his hand out, the pain was more than he could bear. He began to struggle, but in moments he was almost out of breath.

Bill's friend, Pete Rossi, was also collecting fishes nearby. Pete saw Bill struggling and swam to the rescue. He thrust the handle of his net into the hole, again and again. Finally Bill's hand was released. With the last of his strength, Bill pushed to the surface and gasped for air. The palm of his hand and several of his fingers were badly cut. A doctor sewed many stitches in the hand.

Both Bill and Pete knew that Bill had done a very foolish thing. One of the basic rules of skin diving is "Never put your hand in a dark hole." Deadly moray eels may live in those holes.

Green Moray Eel

Moray eels are very strong fishes with small sharp teeth and very bad tempers. They live in holes and caves, with their heads just out of sight. When an unsuspecting fish swims by, the moray grabs it quickly and pulls the victim into the hole. People are bitten only if they place a hand or foot in or near a hole in which a moray eel lives. The result can be fatal, for the eel just hangs on, with its strong body tightly twisted in the hole. Some swimmers have drowned before they could set themselves free. Others, although they have lived to tell of their meeting with a moray eel, have received very serious wounds.

Many kinds of moray eels are found in warm oceans around the world. In the United States they are found along the coast of Florida, in the Gulf of Mexico, and off Southern California, wherever there are coral reefs or rock formations.

Barracudas are found in warm ocean waters all over the world. They occur all year round off the coasts of Florida and Southern California. In summer they move farther north. These fishes are the lone wolves of the sea, for the large ones usually travel alone. They are always on the lookout for something to eat.

A barracuda rests quietly in the water until some flashing movement attracts its attention. If the moving thing appears good to eat, the barracuda swims around the victim, studying it carefully. Then, with a lightning-fast motion, the barracuda takes a quick, clean bite. A barracuda has many needle-like teeth.

Experienced divers often fear barracudas more than sharks, even though barracudas seldom grow to more than six feet. Many swimmers, with their moving legs and arms flashing in the clear ocean water, have attracted barracudas. No one is ever killed outright by a barracuda bite. But since the bite is usually a large one, a victim is likely to bleed to death if he cannot get help in a short time.

Pacific Barracuda

Great Barracuda

CHAPTER THREE

Say's Stingray

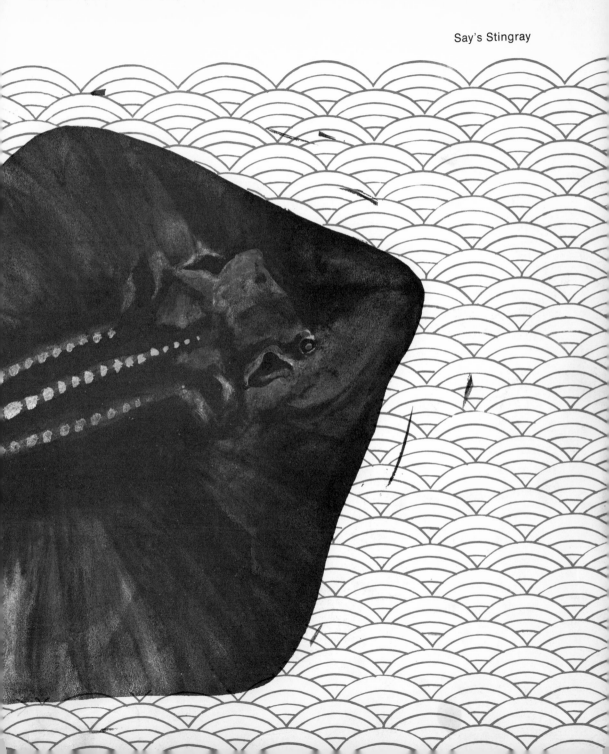

Jim Parsons was sitting on a dock beside a cool New England lake, fishing with a cane pole. The bobber on his line bobbed a few times. Jim was tempted to pull the line in at once, but he remembered his dad's advice: "Give them time to take it. Wait for the bobber to go under and stay under."

The bobber ducked again and stayed under. The line sliced through the water as a fish ran with the bait. Jim pulled hard and a nice bullhead catfish landed on the dock.

As Jim picked the catfish up, the fish raised the fin on its back and the two fins on its sides. Jim dropped the bullhead with a loud "Ouch!" In the center of Jim's hand there were three round holes. The hand was sore for several days. Jim had learned a lesson that he would remember all his life: catfish must be handled very carefully. They have sharp spines in their fins. Many kinds of catfish even have poisonous glands beneath some of the spines.

While no one ever dies from catfish injuries, the wound is more painful than a bee sting. Madtoms, small catfish that are found in streams over most of the United States, give the most painful stings of all. Madtoms make very interesting aquarium pets, but they should never be handled.

Round Stingray

Stingrays

Unlike their fierce cousins the sharks, stingrays are shy fishes. They use their dangerous stingers, not to harm their victims, but to protect themselves from their enemies. Only by accident does a person get stung.

There are many kinds of stingrays in the world. Several kinds are found along the coasts of North America. They are flat fishes, with a long, whip-like tail. On the tail is a sharp stiff spine, the stinger. Along the spine are rows of barbs, like the barb on a fish hook. At the base of the spine is a little sac filled with poison. Some stingrays also have rows of sharp "teeth" along the tail.

The stingray lies quietly on the bottom. If a larger fish attacks it, or if a man accidentally steps on it, the stingray flips its tail against the attacker or against the man's foot. The sharp spine pierces the flesh and poison is forced out of the sac. Since the spine is covered with barbs, it sticks very firmly in the wound and breaks off when the stingray moves its tail away. If the victim is a person, he falls in great pain. If he cannot get help from a doctor, the victim suffers for weeks until the wound heals or until he dies. When a stingray loses its spine, it soon grows a new one.

Most stingrays live in the ocean, but in South America, where so many odd and dangerous fishes live, there are fresh-water stingrays.

Indians are very careful about walking in water in their bare feet. But even with care, many Indians and many visitors from the outside world have received painful stings from fresh-water stingrays.

Fresh-water Stingray

The Lionfish, or Turkey Fish

The lionfish is another famous stinging fish. Just about 12 inches in length, it is found along the coral reefs of the South Pacific Ocean. It is colored in orange and white stripes almost brighter than an artist could paint. All of its fins look like long, brightly colored feathers.

The lionfish is dangerous to touch, for hidden inside each bright "feather" is a long, sharp spine. At the base of each spine is a little sac of poison. When the lionfish is attacked, it spreads its fins and stands its ground. If the fins are touched, the attacker receives a very painful wound.

Many people have brushed against a lionfish and have lived to regret it. It is said that a wound from a lionfish can paralyze a man's arm or leg for several weeks.

Lionfish are sometimes kept in home aquariums because of their great beauty. They seem to live very well in captivity, if the aquarist has a large supply of small fishes to feed them. Of course, this is one pet that must never be petted!

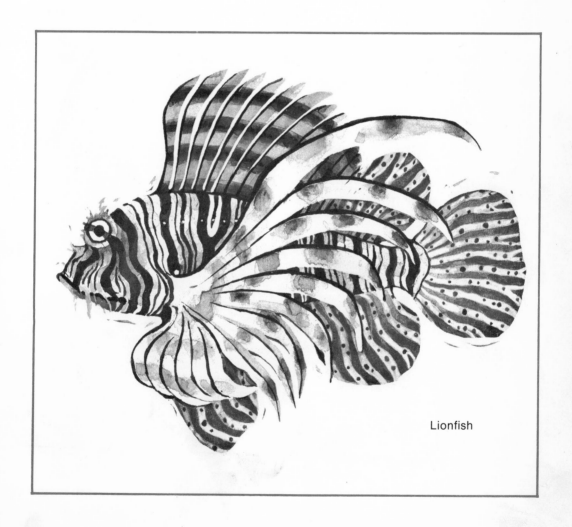

Lionfish

The Deadly Stonefish

A cousin of the lionfish is said to have the most deadly poison of any fish in the world. It is the stonefish of the South Pacific and Indian Oceans. This homely, dull-colored fish lives partly buried on the bottom, where it is almost impossible to see. It has many short, sharp spines, which are held up stiffly whenever the fish senses danger. Any unsuspecting swimmer who steps on a stonefish is in serious trouble, because the poison is extremely fast-acting. It is sometimes fatal within a few hours.

Stonefish

Other Relatives of the Lionfish

The lionfish has many cousins around the world. All of these relatives, including the lionfish, belong to a family of fishes called scorpionfishes. (The scorpion is a land-dwelling relative of insects and crabs, and it has a powerful stinger in its tail.) The scorpionfishes are named for scorpions because all of these fishes have sharp spines that sting. Many kinds of scorpionfishes have poison glands at the base of their spines.

The California scorpionfish, which is sometimes caught by fishermen, is nearly as poisonous as the lionfish. Any fisherman on the Pacific coast who catches a scorpionfish should remove it from the hook very carefully!

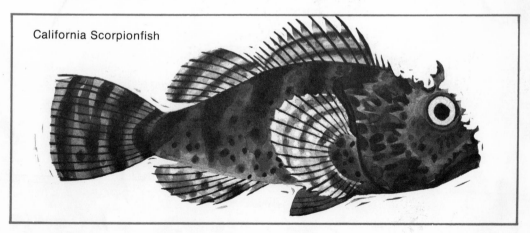

California Scorpionfish

CHAPTER FOUR

Northern Puffer (normal)

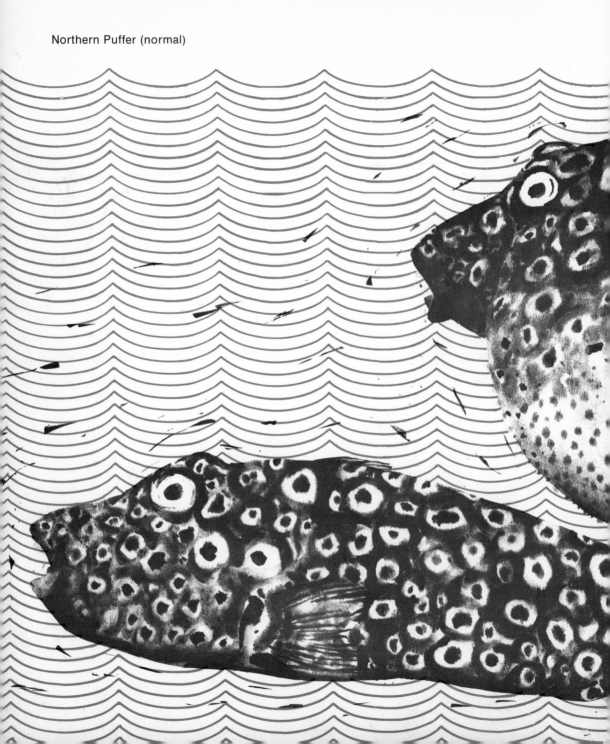

Northern Puffer (inflated)

If you have fished for puffers, or blowfish, you know how they get their name. When puffers are pulled from the water, they take in great gulps of air until they look like a balloon with eyes and a short tail. In water, puffers puff up with water when a larger fish attacks them. Then they are often much too big to be eaten. When the danger passes, they let out the water and return to their normal size.

The puffers found along the eastern coast of North America are very good to eat. But the puffers from some other parts of the world contain a very strong poison called tetrodotoxin. Studies have proven that most of the poison is in the puffers' internal organs.

In some countries puffers are eaten even though it is well known that they may be poisonous. The Japanese make a dish from puffers called fugu. If the puffers are carefully cleaned, they are safe to eat, but each year some Japanese people become sick from eating carelessly prepared fugu. A few people die.

Very, very few fishes are dangerous to man because they are poisonous to eat. In general, it is safe to say that nearly all fishes may be eaten. Some fishes taste better than others, however, and that is the real basis for deciding if a fish is good to eat. In fact, there are so few poisonous to eat fishes that, in addition to puffers, only two others will be mentioned.

In the waters of the South Pacific there is a fish called the oil fish. If the flesh of this fish is eaten it causes very bad stomach pains.

The oil fish isn't all bad, however. Natives have learned that a small amount of juice from an oil fish is a useful medicine.

You have already met the barracuda, which is one of the dangerous biting fishes. Barracuda meat is generally thought to be quite tasty and good to eat. But some cases of poisoning have been reported. Even though scientists have discovered many things about the fishes that are dangerous to man, scientists really aren't certain why barracuda meat may be poisonous. This is just one of the mysteries still to be solved.

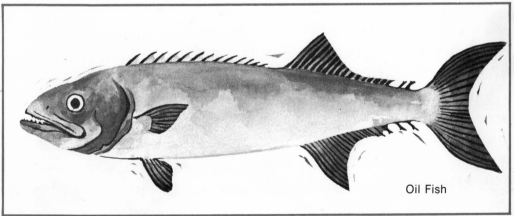
Oil Fish

Mako Shark

INDEX

THE AUTHOR

THE ARTISTS

Alan Mark Fletcher's knowledge of the dangerous fishes of South America is first-hand; he has made at least ten expeditions into the jungle to study and gather material for books, articles, and lectures. In addition, he spent nine years editing *The Aquarium,* a monthly hobby magazine. Mr. Fletcher is a biology graduate of Juniata College and has taught science at the Stony Brook School for Boys on Long Island and Shady Grove Junior High School in Ambler, Pennsylvania. At the present time, Mr. Fletcher is associated with Cornell University. He lives in Ithaca, New York, with his wife and four daughters.

Jane Teiko Oka and *Willi Baum,* both distinguished graphic designers, have combined their talents to create illustrations which are both documentary and decorative. They used the resources of the Steinhart Aquarium in San Francisco to assure that their drawings of fishes would be wholly accurate.

Jane Teiko Oka numbers three other books for children in her illustration credits. A Fulbright Fellow with a year's study in Japan, she likes outdoor sports and is an avid skier.

Willi Baum received his artistic training in Bern, Switzerland. After working in advertising as an artist and art director, he became a well-known and well-regarded illustrator of children's literature. Mr. Baum has illustrated two other Addison-Wesley juvenile books, THE MIRACLE OF THE MOUNTAIN and his own BIRDS OF A FEATHER.